Count On Us

A Tennessee Number Book

Written by Michael Shoulders and Illustrated by Bruce Langton

Sleeping Bear Press
2395 South Huron Parkway
Suite 200
Ann Arbor, MI 48104
www.sleepingbearpress.com

Printed and bound in the United States.

10 9 8 7 6 5 4 3

Count on us : a Tennessee number book / written by Michael Shoulders ;
illustrated by Bruce Langton.
p. cm.
Summary: Presents short rhymes about numbers of objects from
one through 100 and provides information about the Tennessee
natural history and social studies topics that the objects represent.
ISBN 1-58536-131-3
1. Tennessee-Juvenile literature. 2. Counting-Juvenile literature.
[1. Tennessee. 2. Counting.] I. Langton, Bruce, ill. II. Title.
F436.3 .S53 2003
976.8--dc21   2003008947

For Jason—who believes in the magic of numbers.

MIKE

෴

*This book is for all children that have the
motivation and desire to become book illustrators.
Through hard work & determination your
dreams will come true as mine did.*

*My thanks to Sleeping Bear Press and
Mike Shoulders for all their professional help
to bring another wonderful book to life.*

*My love for my family goes without saying.
Thanks to Rebecca, Brett, and Rory.*

BRUCE

Fall Creek Falls State Park is located in Bledsoe and Van Buren counties. Nature lovers flock to the park to enjoy the wealth of wildlife and scenery found there. Fall Creek Falls, one of several falls in the park, is over 250 feet tall. That makes it the tallest waterfall in the eastern half of the United States. Usually, there is only one waterfall in this location. However, when rain is abundant, a second fall flows to the right of the main waterfall.

Visitors to Fall Creek Falls State Park may hike a walking trail to the bottom of the gorge for a spectacular view. Other trails in the park lead to other cascades, past beautiful streams, over a swinging bridge, and through beautiful gorges.

one

1

1 spectacular waterfall
such beauty rare to see.
The tallest falls east of the Rockies
is found in Tennessee!

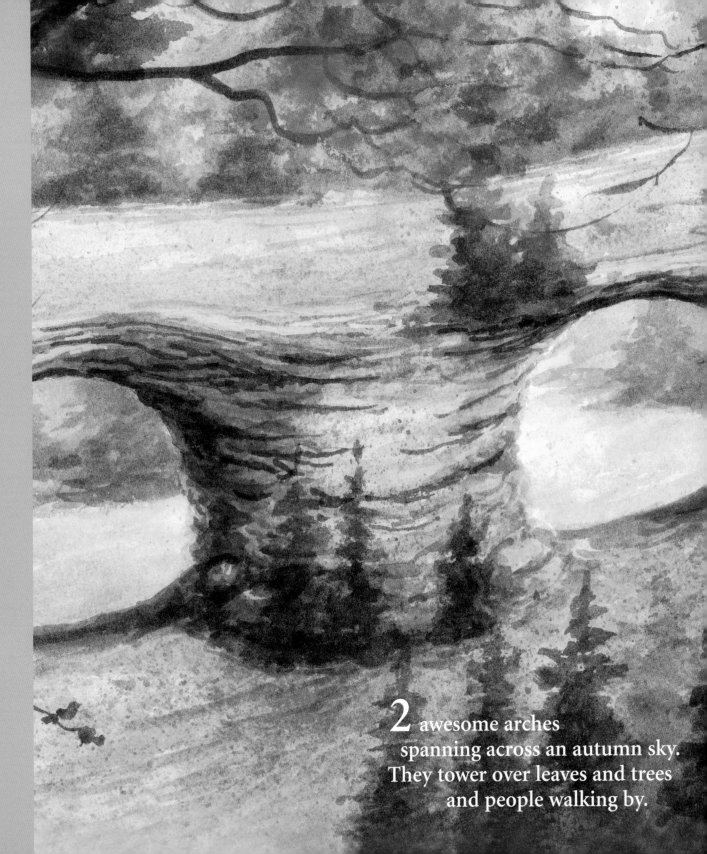

Millions of years ago, an ocean covered the area around Oneida, Tennessee. Sandstone formed beneath a covering of conglomerate rock. Over time, this area lifted above sea level. Wind and rain eroded the sandstone beneath the conglomerate. This erosion of sandstone created many unusual land-forms. "Twin Arches" is located in Big South Fork River and Recreation Area, a few miles from Oneida. They are just one of the many magnificent rock for-mations found here.

two

2

2 awesome arches
spanning across an autumn sky.
They tower over leaves and trees
and people walking by.

Tennessee walking horses are gentle animals. Their legs can easily move with long strides. These horses perform three different gaits (or walks): the flat foot walk, running walk, and the canter. The flat foot walk is a fast, long-reaching walk that can move the horse from four to eight miles an hour. The running walk is similar to the flat foot walk but faster, with some horses running 10-20 miles an hour. The canter is a relaxed gallop.

The annual Tennessee Walking Horse National Celebration is one of the largest horse shows in the world. Henry Davis began the competition in 1939. The winning horse is crowned "The World Grand Champion."

three
3

3 Tennessee walking horses
stepping straight and proud.
A blue ribbon for the champion
as cheers ring from the crowd.

The United States Treasury began minting commemorative quarters for the 50 states in 1999. Tennessee's quarter was the 16th to be released because Tennessee became the 16th state on June 1, 1796. By 2008, all 50 state quarters will be in circulation.

The quarter representing the Volunteer State depicts a fiddle, a guitar, and a horn placed near three stars. The horn reminds us of W.C. Handy, "The Blues," and Memphis. The fiddle pays homage to the Appalachian music of East Tennessee, and the guitar honors the roots of country music in Middle Tennessee. Three stars also appear on the Tennessee flag and represent the three geographic regions of the state.

four

4

4 bright and shiny quarters
with a guitar, a horn, and fiddle
represent music of Tennessee
from the east, the west, and middle.

Tourists from all over the United States visit the Peabody Hotel in Memphis. They don't necessarily come to stay. Many come to watch the famous parade of the Peabody Ducks. Five mallard ducks, which include four hens and one drake, live in the fancy Duck Palace located on the roof of the hotel. Each morning, at 11:00 a.m., the Duckmaster and an Honorary Duckmaster come down the elevator and lead the ducks to the marble fountain in the Grand Lobby. The mallards waddle to the fountain on a red carpet while one of John Philip Sousa's marches plays in the background. At 5:00 p.m., spectators return to watch the ducks repeat the parade back to their home on the roof.

five

5

5 perky Peabody Ducks
all marching in a row.
Waddling down the carpet and
"splash!" in the water they go.

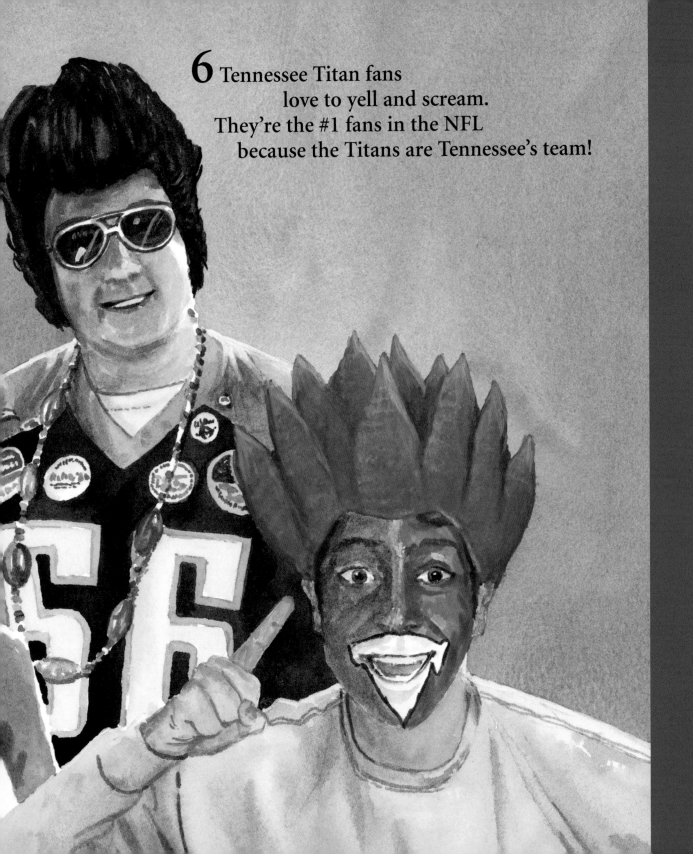

6 Tennessee Titan fans
love to yell and scream.
They're the #1 fans in the NFL
because the Titans are Tennessee's team!

The Tennessee Titans, a team in the National Football League, play their games in Nashville. The stadium is located on the east bank of the Cumberland River and seats over 67,000 screaming fans! The Titan fans are considered some of the most loyal and devoted fans in the NFL.

The Tennessee Titan symbol is a ball of flames with a "T" and three stars. Many Titan fans wear flame wigs to games and dress in red, white, and blue. Die-hard fans are affectionately called "Flame Heads!"

six

6

Reelfoot Lake is one of Tennessee's most unusual natural wonders. It was formed on December 16, 1811 after a severe earthquake struck northwest Tennessee. The earthquake caused a large land area in Obion County to sink several feet. The Mississippi River flowed backward to fill in the depression and Reelfoot Lake was formed. The lake covers 14,500 acres. During the winter season, Reelfoot Lake is home to the largest population of American bald eagles in the eastern United States. Tourists come equipped with binoculars and cameras hoping to spy a mother eagle and her nest of young.

seven

7 elegant eagles,
some soaring near their nest,
find raising chicks is lots of work.
It's time to take a rest!

Missouri

Kentucky

8 states border the Volunteer State.
Arkansas is to our west.
Kentucky's our neighbor to the north.
Now can you name the rest?

Arkansas

TENNESSEE

Mississippi

Alabama

Virginia

North Carolina

Georgia

No state has more neighbors than Tennessee. Missouri ties Tennessee with eight state neighbors. Parts of the Volunteer State touch:

Kentucky: the Bluegrass State
Virginia: the Old Dominion State
North Carolina: the Tarheel State
Georgia: the Peach Tree State
Alabama: the Yellowhammer State
Mississippi: the Magnolia State
Arkansas: the Natural State
Missouri: the Show Me State

eight
8

The channel catfish is Tennessee's state commercial fish. They live in fast moving, cool streams. The channel cat has eight sensory barbels or "feelers" around its mouth that look like cat whiskers. The barbels help the catfish find food at night. Catfish make their nests in tunnels in stream banks or under logs.

Paris, Tennessee is home to the "World's Largest Fish Fry," held every year during the last week of April. Over 12,500 pounds of fish are served to catfish enthusiasts every year! One highlight of the fish fry is the catfish races. Catfish are placed in long clear troughs. The first catfish to swim to the other end of the trough wins. If it's a close race, the fish might win by a whisker!

nine

9

5 chubby channel cats
swimming in a brook.
They're searching for a meal to eat.
Watch out for the hook!

10 flickering fireflies
lighting up the night.
	Dancing on a moonless eve,
catch them in mid-flight.

Fireflies are one of four Tennessee state insects. They are not flies at all, but beetles! Fireflies have special light organs on the underside of their abdomens. These light organs display a heatless light through chemical reactions. It is believed that fireflies flash to warn predators of their bitter taste. But that doesn't stop some frogs from eating them. Fireflies only live for two months...after that... it's lights out!

ten
10

Another of Tennessee's state insects is a delightful friend to have in a garden. This beetle eats large numbers of plant-eating insects, particularly aphids. Female beetles eat as many as 75 aphids a day. Smaller male beetles eat up to 40 per day.

Ladybugs live in trees, shrubs, fields, and even houses. The red and black colors of the beetles protect them from birds because birds have learned that insects with those colors usually taste bad. Ladybugs are smart insects! They "play dead" when attacked by birds because they know many predators will not eat an insect that doesn't move!

eleven
11

11 lovely ladybugs
are resting on a vine.
To have one land upon your hand
is considered a lucky sign.

The Chattanooga Bakery in Chattanooga, Tennessee began making the MoonPie in 1917. Legend has it Mr. Earl Mitchell Sr. asked some coal miners what they wanted to eat for a snack. They told Mr. Mitchell they needed something solid and filling. He asked them how big the snack should be. A miner responded by showing, with his hands, a circle the size of the full moon in the sky that night. The baker was already dipping graham crackers in marshmallow. Mr. Mitchell suggested that another cookie be added and that it be dipped in chocolate. MoonPies come in several sizes: double-decker, single-decker, and mini. Today, MoonPies are coated in three flavors: chocolate, banana, and vanilla.

twelve
12

12 MoonPies stacked in a box.
Are you hungry for a bite?
The "double-decker" is perfect for
a hardy appetite!

20 race cars on a track—
chasing past the crowd.
Roaring, soaring, booming, zooming,
20 race cars can be loud!

The Bristol Motor Speedway is a favorite stop for NASCAR fans. With audiences of over 160,000, racing events held here support the largest crowds for any sporting event in Tennessee. The racetrack was built in 1961 on the site of a dairy farm. The track is exactly .533 miles long or just over a half-mile. It is 40 feet wide on the straightaways and 60 feet wide in the turns. Cars zoom past spectators at speeds of over 100 miles per hour.

Counting to 20 is easy to do.
Can you do it two-by-two?
The colors can help you—full speed ahead.
Begin your counting with the color red.

twenty

20

The passionflower is Tennessee's official state wildflower. Its lemon scented purple flowers attach to vines that grow easily in different types of terrain throughout the state. The fruit of the plant is a berry also called the water lemon or maypop. It is round with a tart flavor and makes a loud popping sound when crushed.

Early Native Americans prized the passionflower as the most beautiful of the flowers. The Indians used the crushed leaves of the passionflower to help heal cuts and bruises. The vines were brewed for tea and were said to have had a calming effect.

30 purple passionflowers
make this scene complete.
The vines of our state wildflower grow
to a length of 30 feet!

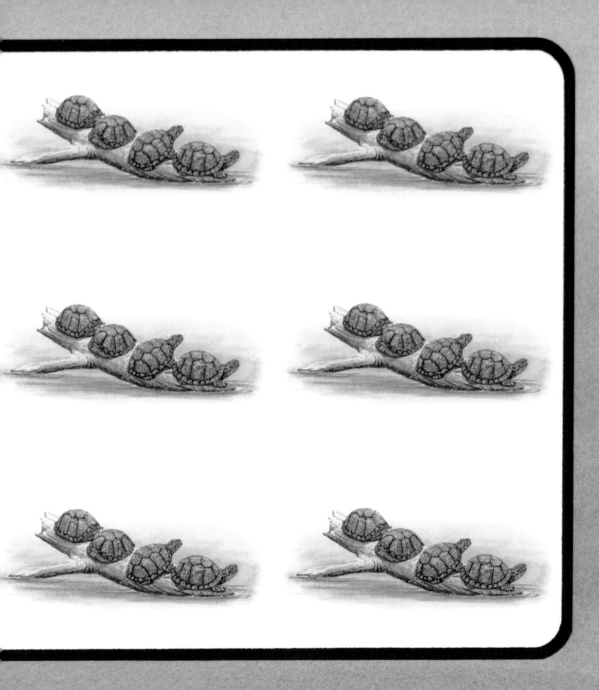

The 99th General Assembly designated the Eastern Box Turtle, *Terrapene carolina*, as the Volunteer State's official state reptile in 1995. This peaceful creature grows to a length of between 5 and 6 inches and has been known to live to the ripe old age of 60.

The top shell of the Eastern Box Turtle is called a carapace. It is black, brown, tan, or olive with splotches of yellow, orange, and red. The bottom shell is called a plastron. It is hinged to allow the shell to close much like a box when the turtle is frightened

Although quite shy, spring and summer showers bring box turtles out of their hiding spots in search of drink and food. Box turtles are omnivorous, which means they eat a variety of plants and animals.

forty

40

40 box turtles sitting in rows
have found a watering place!
Turtles know when the going gets tough—
Slow and steady wins every race.

The largemouth bass is Tennessee's official state game fish. The largemouth bass eats minnows and small bluegill. They hide near rocks and tree logs to capture unsuspecting prey. Largemouth bass are called game fish because they are hard to catch yet quite tasty!

Largemouth bass can be studied up close at the Tennessee State Aquarium in Chattanooga. It is the largest fresh-water aquarium in the world. Visitors observe water forming a stream in the Appalachian Mountains and follow it through exhibits as it eventually flows into the Gulf of Mexico. Along the way, plants and animals are viewed in their freshwater habitats.

fifty
50

50 fish native to Tennessee
swimming all about:
perch, brim, crappie, largemouth bass,
and colorful rainbow trout.

60 snow-white cotton balls
   glued upon six sheep.
Leave them alone and they'll come home
      to their owner: Little Bo Peep!

Cotton is Tennessee's top agricultural product. Cotton requires a temperate climate. The delta region of southwest Tennessee furnishes the appropriate conditions and adequate water supply. Memphis, with the Mississippi River nearby, provides a perfect transportation port.

Cotton seeds are planted in February. The warm summer days of June help the white cotton blossoms to sprout. After the blossom stage, bolls appear and continue to grow until fall's first frost. The hard, triangular shaped bolls burst and white cotton is exposed. A cotton gin separates the seed from the soft balls of cotton. The cotton is cleaned, pressed, and sent to market.

sixty
60

Tennessee is proud to be the home for two car manufacturing plants. The Nissan plant in Smyrna is the largest auto manufacturing plant under one roof. The first Nissan sedan was manufactured in 1992.

The Saturn plant is situated in Spring Hill on a 2,400 acre "green field" away from large cities. Employees use a team approach and have built more than 2 million Saturn cars.

seventy

70

70 cars off the assembly line
polished and brand new.
Some are red, some are green,
and some are deep sky-blue.

80 colorful writing pencils,
sharp and looking pretty.
Millions of pencils are made each day
in Shelbyville, "The Pencil City."

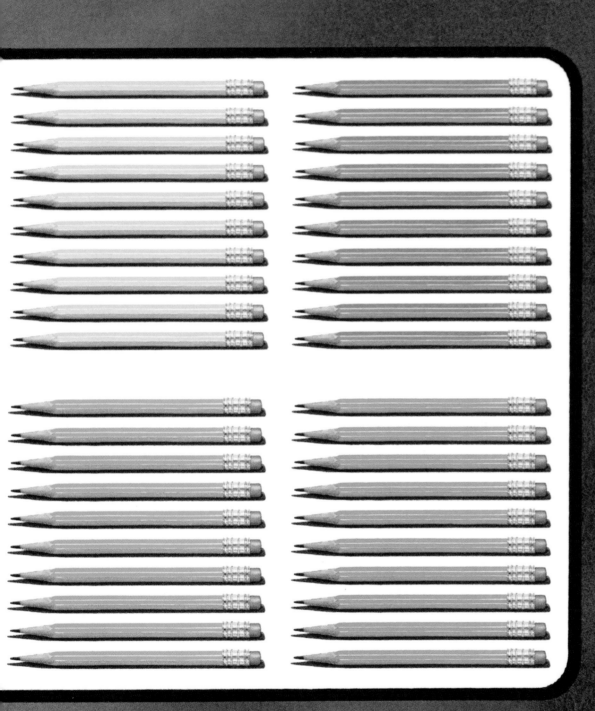

Pencils are the world's number-one writing tool. The first known wooden pencil dates back to the mid-1500s. Graphite was inserted into hollowed-out sticks and the first wooden pencil was born.

Over 2 billion pencils are used in the United States every year. One pencil can write 45,000 words or make a single line 35 miles long! Because so many pencils were made in Shelbyville, in 1950 Governor Buford Ellington named that town the "Pencil City." Today, millions of pencils are made every day there.

eighty
80

Tennessee's official state gem is the freshwater pearl. Unlike cultured pearls, which are partially man-made, freshwater pearls are created naturally from mussels living in rivers and streams. Freshwater pearls come in many different shapes and colors. "Pearling" was a favorite hobby until the mid-twentieth century. Dams and toxic waste affected the shallow breeding grounds of mussels and they are not as plentiful today. Collected river pearls are made into rings, cuff links, and other jewelry.

ninety
90

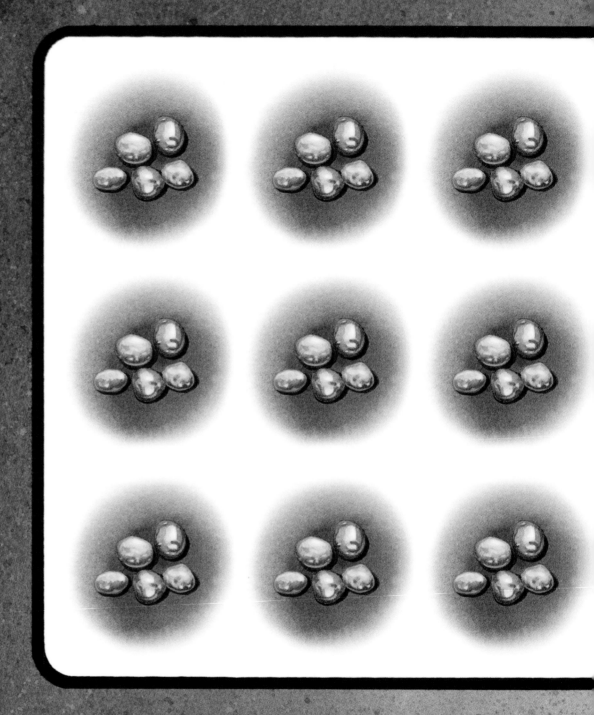

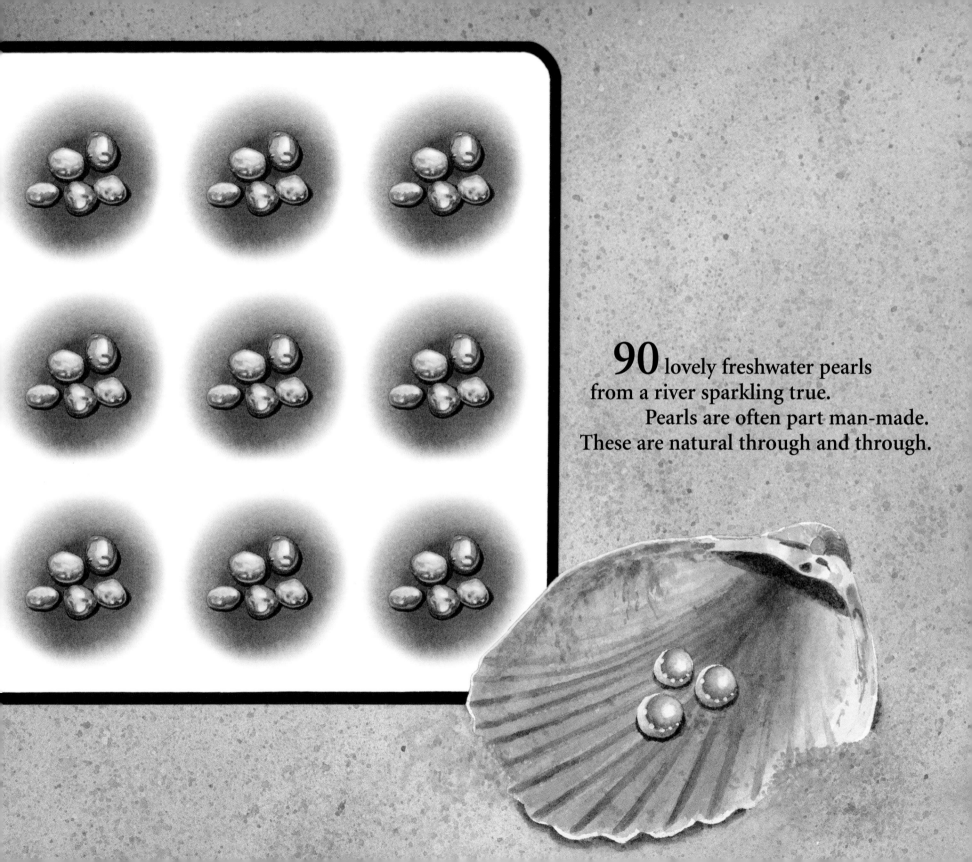

90 lovely freshwater pearls
from a river sparkling true.
Pearls are often part man-made.
These are natural through and through.

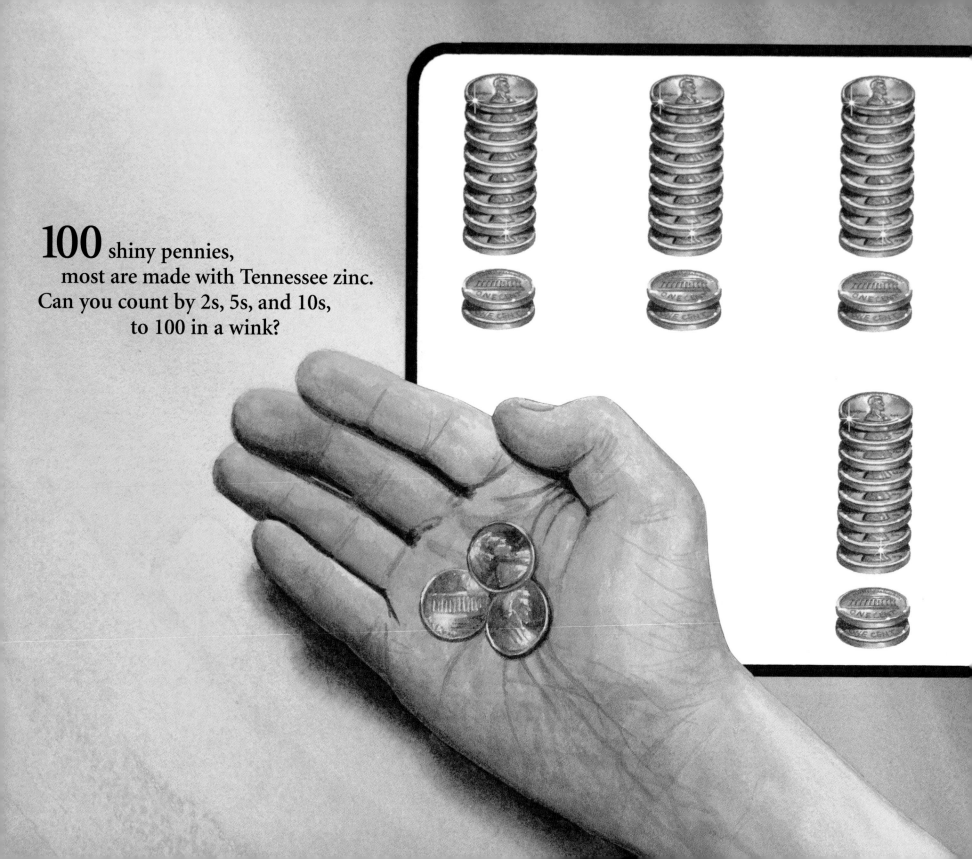

100 shiny pennies,
most are made with Tennessee zinc.
Can you count by 2s, 5s, and 10s,
to 100 in a wink?

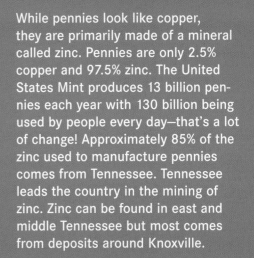

While pennies look like copper, they are primarily made of a mineral called zinc. Pennies are only 2.5% copper and 97.5% zinc. The United States Mint produces 13 billion pennies each year with 130 billion being used by people every day—that's a lot of change! Approximately 85% of the zinc used to manufacture pennies comes from Tennessee. Tennessee leads the country in the mining of zinc. Zinc can be found in east and middle Tennessee but most comes from deposits around Knoxville.

one
hundred
100

Michael Shoulders

Michael Shoulders is a Federal Programs Supervisor and has worked for the Clarksville-Montgomery County School System for twenty-eight years. His "Story Time" column appears every week in the *Clarksville-Leaf Chronicle*. Michael enjoys traveling and speaking to educators and children about writing and books. Michael lives in Clarksville, Tennessee and he and his wife, Debbie, have three children, Jason, Ryan, and Meghann, and a standard poodle named Hershey.

Bruce Langton

Bruce was born in Minnesota and grew up on a lake in Wisconsin where he spent numerous hours enjoying and observing nature. His father was a great outdoorsman and Bruce learned many aspects about hunting, fishing, and preserving nature through conservation. Today Bruce teaches his two sons what was handed down from his father through fly-fishing and his art. Bruce has also helped raise many thousands of dollars for conservation and the preservation of nature.

Illustrating children's books, giving school presentations, teaching children how to draw and helping to teach children Kyokushinkai Karate are all a part of Bruce's plan in life to be a well-rounded father, husband, and friend to people and family that surround him.

Today, Bruce resides in Indiana with his wife Rebecca and two sons, Brett and Rory.